Sometimes I fall asleep on the sofa

Milla Tebbs

Published by Big White Shed, Nottingham, England
ISBN 978-1-9164035-0-5
Printed and bound by Booksfactory EU
Cover design by Laura Nielsen
Edited by Chris McLoughlin

"When my mouth forgets how to language,
I sentence with my hands"
-Shinji Moon

Contents

Carry Me Sideways

I don't want to be vertical any longer than I have to be.
Keep me parallel to the ground
so that the contents of my soul are distributed evenly;
let the darkness in my mind corrupt the rest of my body.

Keep me preserved like a stuffed animal but still breathing.
The weight of my problems needs to be shared equally,
if I am to function in any other way than off
                                                    balance.

Please, allow me to stay horizontal.
In my current upright state I am struggling.
Functioning is difficult when you're as uneven as a country road
- how am I to keep on the straight and narrow
when potholes are emerging in the most unlikely of places?
I can't even complain because many are self-inflicted.

I'm hoping that things will make more sense
if I change my position.
Sometimes, to find a solution we must turn things on their head.
So, being carried sideways may improve my situation, or at least
that way I can close my eyes and pretend
I'm tucked up in bed.

Fingerprints

I don't know
if the police will find fingerprints,
but I can feel them;
in the creases of my underwear
that you threw carelessly onto the carpet,
and on my old laptop
(you didn't see as worthy enough to steal.)

I can sense your touch;
where you rummaged for value
in things only sentimental.
My freshly washed sheets seem foreign to me;
how is it that I feel like the intruder,
when I'm the innocent intrudee?

I question your dedication
to the violation of our home
when you fed my cat
even if only to shut her up.
This level of compassion
is not something I would associate
with someone who takes a christening bracelet
my great grandad Paddy
gave my sister when she was born.
It shouldn't matter that it's never been worn
apart from when he put it on her child-thin wrist.
If anything, that makes it more precious;
as his fingers now buried in the ground
were probably the last to touch it
before you thought it was gold you found.

I can't believe you missed my camera
what kind of amateur burglar
doesn't check the windowsill?
But takes a vibrator

(even if only for the thrill)
that's pretty grim.
I guess that isn't such a problem for someone
who will happily kick their way into a home,
take what they want
and leave -
for the police to search with a fine-tooth comb.

I doubt we'll ever find out who you are,
let alone retrieve our belongings
but they both seem like menial things
in comparison to the intrusion.
Because I can see where your fingers
pulled open every drawer,
your eyes saw money signs reflected in silver.

I'm left with nothing but confusion
as to whether you've done this before.
Because nothing was broken;
despite the vases precariously placed
on shelves far too thin,
the PlayStation 4 was left untouched.

Sure, you waited till no one was in
but I still can't believe you fed my cat
when you could just as easily have *done her in!*
So, I am thankful for that
but I am not thankful for
how you've made me feel unsafe
in my own home -
knowing that a stranger has had free roam.

I now have 3 keys to my front door
but I'm pretty sure
that even if I had 3 more,
I could still feel your fingerprints
in my underwear drawer.

How Much for Anal?

I pride myself on not being judgmental, so
I hide my wincing
behind a twitching
pretending to have something in my eye
when in fact
I am afraid.

At 8:23 in the evening
my heart beat has increased at the
mere sight of the group
that even though
I've never clapped eyes on -
I feel like I've seen before.
A group of 6ft teenage boys
with the smell of testosterone
as poignant as
the cigarette one just put out
on another's shoe.

Their circle a sea of Nike and Adidas
that I would hate to drown in.
I am out of my depth
it is 8:23 in the evening
and I am inadvertently judging them.

My body tenses at the sight
of their hands down their joggers,
because their frames match that
of the one who approached me
in an almost identical situation,
not that I know if it was 8:23 or not,
but it was evening.
I was sat in the square
as the sun set, having a fag
as I waited for my bus -

"How much for anal?"

suddenly I'm not the only judgmental one.
I'll never know
if they were taking the piss
or genuinely thought
I was a prostitute,
and every time I tell this story
I'm asked what I was wearing.

As if the hole in my fishnets
is an invitation
and the skirt riding up my thigh
the starter for a dirty conversation.
So, maybe I shouldn't pride myself
on not being judgmental
but can you blame me? When
it is 8:23 in the evening and
I feel vulnerable.

I'm Not All That Fond of People

I'm not all that fond of people
the unspoken language of the human body
is one that I am far from fluent in but wish to learn.
Because I'm sick of being a tourist
among my own species and I don't know
where to begin because, I've spent my life
trying to conform to normality but
I never got very far.
My differences were always mistaken for insanity
so, I think I need a new introduction.
Why doesn't life come with a manual
for those of us who struggle to function?

I'm not all that fond of people
because I don't understand them - how sometimes
they say things they don't mean
for comic affect and all of a sudden
I'm the butt of their jokes for taking it literally.
Unknown territory is my biggest fear
that I need to conquer If I'm to survive -
It's not a case of 'if' but 'when' because this alienation
is eating me alive.

But I'm not all that fond of people
even though I'm biologically one myself
with the same number of cells as Beyoncé.
I still feel like an outsider
unable to relate to anyone else;
regardless of what the genetics say.

I'm not all that fond of people
but leave me with something
furry and four-legged and
I am more than comfortable.
Because animals don't judge you

(except cats)
even if they did
there's not much they can do,
when their evolution was stunted
by the domestication forced on them
by our selfish human population.

I'm not all that fond of people
the way their words cut like a cheese knife,
their tongues razor blades
and the air they breathe a sharpener.

I'm not all that fond of people
whose declarations are cheesy;
over-used lines
smeared with insincerity
do nothing for me.

I'm not all that fond of people
the human mind is a maze
that I regularly get lost in
and find myself uncomfortable.

I'm not all that fond of people
who cut you down like a tree trunk
in southern America
then expect you to build yourself back up
without fertiliser.

I'm not all that fond of people
who I can't read.
I can only read books.

I'm not all that fond of people
the unspoken language of the human body
is still a mystery to me,
but I'm willing to open my eyes and see

that maybe it's not that
I'm not all that fond of people,
people just aren't all that fond of me.

An Ode to Noses

When asked why I love noses
I am stumped
and then mutter –

"They're the centre of the face."

To which I get no backlash
because you can't argue
with the geography of facial features.

       nose
The way the   sticks out
further than any other
speaks volumes to me.

If you tell someone they have a nice nose
they scrunch it up like a crisp packet,
and there's nothing more beautiful to me
than a blush in the nasal area.

~~I Love You~~

You tell me not to say it
So, I don't -
Won't let the words leave my lips
or the syllables penetrate
the space between us.

But we can both feel them;
their weight hangs in the air
between my eye
and your avoiding stare
like a question mark,
dangles on a string
from your mouth to mine
that you cut without thought.

And those words
you never wanted to hear
fall silent, dormant
in their missed opportunity,
and I wonder
what you want from me
am I just another
sleazy hotel hook-up,
a dirty pair of suspenders
laddered with false promises?
Because I thought I was more,
thought those words
meant something more,
meant something.

Because you said them once
in hushed declarations, and again
in sincere exclamations.

But me,
I'm not allowed to say them;
those words can't leave my lips -
you won't let them.
The double standards are strangling
as the words choke me -
get stuck in my throat
by your doubt and my chapped lips
call out for them; to be moisturised
by your loveliness once again.

You tell me not to say it
so, I don't
but I wanted to.

Words Don't Belong to Anyone

I've never been the best
at dealing with rejection.
When Molly Spears named Chantelle
as her best friend in year 1
I quickly became closer with Tom,
pretending I'd never been that fussed
about her in the first place.

At 5, I'd already realised
the reality of being
R-E-J-E-C-T-E-D - rejected
was the opposite of humorous.
No one smiles
because they're not enough,
I've never laughed
at having my dreams crushed,
only hidden my tears from view
pretended I don't care
so as not to have to bear
the sympathetic looks.

I was a slightly better liar back then
still crossed my fingers behind my back
but maintained eye contact -
thanks to being forced into youth theatres
from the age of 6.
Though, I'd never have made it as an actress;
my self-esteem wouldn't have been able
to survive an unsuccessful audition,
by my own admission
it was never my bag.
My sister -
she always thrived
in being part of a theatre production
but my skin never grew thick enough

for audience consumption.

So, I waved my white flag
at the age of 16;
started dreaming of
my name down a spine
rather than face on a screen.
'Sticks and stones may break my bones'
but words
are just loans of language,
recycled into different formations
and labelled poetry.

It may feel like it
but is it really a part of me?
When those letters
weren't etched in my throat,
the words
not birthed on my tongue.
We can quote all we like
but words don't really belong
to anyone.

Too Young

If I was given a pound
for every time that I've been told
"you're too young"
to feel a certain way
or for my meaningful thoughts
to be considered profound,
then I'd have more than enough money
to give you all a refund on this book
but unfortunately for you and
consequentially your bank accounts
all I've taken from that patronisation
is a need to prove them all wrong,
to speak up for my generation!

Because I do not need to reach a certain age
before my opinions are validated
as my brain is alive with thoughts and
my heart warm with feelings through which
I've formulated views that are so often
disregarded simply due to my date of birth,
I'm so sick of my age determining my words' worth.

When Anne Frank was 13 when she was
forced into hiding behind a bookcase
because she didn't fit the criteria for
Hitler's Aryan race and yet she wrote
> "In spite of everything I still believe that people
> are really good at heart"
and perhaps it's due to that optimism
that more than 7 decades later
her diary is still considered a work of art.

And don't tell me
that you have to grow up
to change the world when

Malala was 17 when she became
the youngest recipient of the Nobel Peace Prize
for her fight for the right
of all children to education,
after surviving the Taliban's attempt
at her assassination, and she said
>*"I raise my voice not so that I can shout,*
>*but so that those without a voice can be heard."*

And to some that idea may seem absurd
but in a world so contaminated by repression
I encourage those who have the oppurtunity
to be heard to speak without discretion.
Because your voice is important
regardless of how broad your vocabulary
and it is on our shoulders
to help the rest of the world see
that our generation care about more than
just selfies and social media.

Even though I don't sound
like I've swallowed an encyclopaedia
my opinions are still valid
and I will spend my life proving that
I'm an avid believer in the importance of youth.
Yes, I am somewhat biased to tell you the truth but
I still disagree with the premise of being 'too young'
when it is from youth that some
of the bravest souls have sprung
So, I will continue to pour my views into poetry
in the hope that one day it's not written off as naivety.

Death to Normality

Occasionally I struggle to function as a 'normal' person
but I'm not sure I know what constitutes
as the 'normal' version of one anymore,
or even if such a thing exists.
Because I'd like to think that if it did
I would have felt it before
harboured some sense of sanity
that *should* be inside all of us.

Perhaps there's no such thing as normality
just more popular ways of being,
and unless I'm mistaken
I don't recall us all agreeing
to conform to a certain type of living.
So, why should I feel excluded
for functioning in a different way.

Maybe we should all be a little more forgiving
when I'm just trying my best
to make it through each day -
with as much 'normality' as I can muster,
and I apologise if this sounds lacklustre
but just like I'm struggling to function
I'm also finding it hard to articulate
without obstruction
by my wandering thoughts and
inconsistent state of mind.

The Tendency to Presume

I never dreamed I would crave being naive
when knowledge has always been
a much more appealing option for me to perceive.
But *oh*, what I would do to have my biggest worry be
whether to say cheers or thank you
to the bus driver, who'll drop me just outside my house
where it's not technically a bus stop
but it saves me going back on myself 50 feet more.

For some reason, unbeknown to me
I have a tendency to presume that
I must carry the weight of the world in my belly.
When surely it can prop itself up
like it has for the rest of eternity
but *no*,
according to my mind riddled with over thinking
it is my responsibility to stop our race's
inevitable sinking into insanity.
With nothing but over used rhyme
as my not-so-secret-weapon,
unsubtle metaphors constructed to
beckon stability like a nervous dog.

And I don't blame the distrust
when our society seems so built
on a lust for disruption,
but sniff the passion in my palm,
the feelings buried too deep to cause harm
to the exterior skin -
that shows only a pin prick
of what we hold within our souls.

And I know I'll never quite fit the mould
of being *'too cool to care.'*
But if I'm honest I think

I'd much rather dare to believe
that I will never know everything
but I can try to.
Just by living with my eyes wide open,
I can pursue knowledge
in everything I do.

I really wish I knew
how to bring this poem
to an effective conclusion but *no,*
there's still a part of me that craves being naive;
to carry nothing more
than my daily calorie intake in my belly,
but I'm under no illusion that
I wouldn't just be bored stiff living carefree.

Saturday Night/ Sunday Morning City

Saturday night city
stands bolt upright,
awake with intoxicated hook ups
and testosterone-fuelled punch ups.
As we criss-cross the city centre
rolling out of Prinks at 'spoons
where we had a pitcher each,
but by the queue at Rock City
the pavement is doused in Sex on the Beach.
As the bouncers question whether we've 'ad enough
to which follow choruses of
'not yet duck!'

3 hours later,
now in the early hours of the morning
we pile out of the club
avoiding eye contact with those bouncers
who no one would blame for taunting
our now obviously-had-enough-selves.
We stumble past the Lions
desperately trying to make the last bus
with only our badly rolled cigarettes to warm us.

We compare Snapchat stories
and play the who's who of Ryan's
this is where we spotted you;
with lips soaked in Red Stripe
spouting nonsense tangled with laddish tendencies
that only a toilet bowl could undo.
I admired your misplaced confidence -
how logic and the meaning of 'discrete'
ceased to exist
as you tried to steal a guy's skateboard
from beneath his feet.

Sunday morning city
lies silent
one eye half open,
squinting into the sunlight
that retired less than 10 hours ago.
The remnants of that night now swept away,
apart from the fag ends in the bushes of Market Square
and a few sparse cans of Red Stripe
the last of their tribe still intact from yesterday.

We can sit in the same spot
but it all looks different in the daytime,
now the crowds of shoppers are about
we're no longer within earshot
unless 10 feet or fewer from each other.
And the only ones who shout are children
high on nothing but excitement
and too many Mint Imperials from their grandmother.

I can't remember where you were stood
and there are 10x more skateboarders in sight
so, even if the same one were there I highly doubt I could
recognise the one I saw you try to steal last night.

Sleep in Soft Focus

There's something incredibly beautiful
about semi-consciousness
the way closed eyelids twitch as the chest contracts
and limbs look so comfortably uncomfortable.

Everyone looks softer asleep
like somehow, they've reverted back to being new-born
yet to be hardened by our hard world.
Naturally in foetal position, we lie
with faces as squishy as the bouncy castle
at your 7th birthday party.

Mouth slightly ajar
ready to swallow the eight spiders
we're told we eat in our lifetime.
There's no sharp edges when semi-conscious;
no spiky temperament,
or sharp wit,
only the round embrace of a hug
wasted on the vacant space next to us.

When sleeping alone
whose arm will be the lifesaver around our waist?
Will we drown in our dreams,
and not live to remember them with fondness?
Despite this rather depressing possibility
I still find beauty in semi-consciousness.

A Memoir to Metrocigs

Wednesday

I'm no longer angry at you,
that anger has been passed on
to the man in the dodgy off license
who'd run out of my tobacco.
I fear I'm sounding like just another bitter smoker
suffering the effects of the new laws
forcing us into buying bigger quantities
(which in my case just means I smoke more.)

I'm angry at the shop keeper
who sold me yours with a smile
still in the Pall Mall branded packaging-
red, the colour of my eyes after losing you.
Now every time I take a drag
I can taste you
and in each cloud of smoke your absence lingers
like the yellow residue under the nails of
my (and every other smoker's) fingers.

How come after all this hurt,
love is the one thing that stays?

I know we never said it
but I could feel the grasp
pulling our hearts together
as yours resisted,
mine prayed for forever.

So, I'll breathe it out -
exhale it through tobacco tarred breath
and leave my anger with the shop keeper
folded into my ten-pound note
in exchange for all I have left of you.

Tobacco far too twiggy to be considered smooth.
Its harshness mimics what you put me through.

If I'm telling the truth
I know I won't smoke it -
can't bring myself
to take you in my throat another time,
but the anger has been replaced with acceptance
that you're no longer mine.

Saturday

I wrote a poem about you last week
and in it I said 'I'm no longer angry at you'
but now I'm so fucking angry
that I don't think I can bring myself
to speak those words no longer true.

And I know I've always said
'you never have to apologise to me'
but I think now after all you've put me through
the least I deserve is a forced apology -
after you stuck your tongue down another girl's throat
right in front of my face
as if moving on is some sort of fucked up race?

How come after all this hurt,
love is the one thing that stays?

Love
Love-ly,
your favourite adjective.
Everything is lovely to you,
you called me your 'lovely girl'
but there was no love laced into your words.

A Letter to Myself

This is a poem to me
(a younger me)
from me,
girl turned woman
who soon won't have to be careful
about getting home too late or loud
because of the parents.

You may be disappointed to hear that
not much changes
my fringe still needs straightening daily
and I struggle to leave the house bare-faced just as you do.
But my (what was once your) leg hair
has given up defying nature -
no longer grows in opposite directions
or sticks out like it's just endured an electric shock
waiting for a visit from the razor -
it has accepted the divorce.

I've stopped searching for a label
that you spent years gripping onto
like a jet ski, as if,
if you let go you would be washed away by the sea.

I still struggle to get to sleep at night
and even if I persevere with all my might
my body tenses when directed to dance;
as if my limbs and brain are strangers
that only met by coincidence,
just as I hope to reconnect with you –
a girl,
I not only once knew,
but tried to destroy through suicide attempts
and unhealthy relationships.

I will get on my hands and knees to pick up the pieces
of your shattered body
will glaze over the reflection covered in chips
because I know you'd do the same for me
help me up when fallen
if time weren't a barrier I'd hold your hand through torment.
Reminding you that survival is something unquestionable
seeing as I am present.

Sometimes, I fall asleep on the sofa
and like you, I swear I'm only 'resting my eyes'
but its 8pm when I wake up
and I've missed the sun's demise.
I still take sunsets for granted
remember I want to witness it
long since the moon has been planted in the sky
and I still can't say the word goodbye
without wincing
thinking of a lost lover or dead pet.
And I'm yet to cure my millennial obsession with the internet.

But I hope you'd be proud of me
and I'm everything you want to be
juggling functioning with mental stability
has become a natural habit.
But I doubt I'm what you want to see because,
I still don't cut my nails as often as I should
and reminisce about the simplicity of childhood;
age is something I'm yet to succeed at
and self-deprecation is still on my list of things to combat.

But I'm living
I'm breathing through the same lungs you had
they may have taken a battering
but low capacity is their natural habitat
I wish I could see your face when you read this
but as we only have one set of eyes between us

that plausibility seems unlikely.
So, I'll settle for knowing that you read them
let their rhythm penetrate your ears
and the gentle font comfort your eyes
without contamination from tears.

I'll be a woman soon
and not just a 20-year-old
thrown into the world of invoices
without being shown how to set up a direct debit.
It's my responsibility to mould my own world
no more excuses or cries of just being a 'little girl'
I'd wish you luck
but I know how you feel about that
because every time you've been wished luck
it hasn't been granted.
And I don't want to jinx you
or worsen the doubt that was planted
back when positivity was hard to see.
So, just know that you turn out okay
and that I was thinking of you today

all my love,

Me.

Literary Love

Let's make love with our words,
use them to soothe anything that hurts.
Let's italicise our *greatest fears;*
make them seem more accomplishable.
If you choose the right font
anything seems doable
so, choose carefully
the default may be easy
but do you want to be lazy?

Leave ellipses instead of goodbyes…
And never forget to apologise.
~~Tyoies~~ Typos will always happen
we just have to learn to correct them where possible.
An Asterix* isn't cheating
it's just a way of adding more meaning,
an afterthought,
like when you remember a great comeback
hours after the confrontation -
imagine going back and adding it,
not taking away from what you said
just expanding on it.

*Let's draw parentheses around our (beautiful) intimacy,
there's no need for deeper meaning all the time;
a kiss doesn't have to be a sign of commitment,
just a middle finger to resistance.
Let's live through literacy
and take tea breaks during caesuras.

Thank Yous

To Laura Guthrie and David Tebbs (less formally known as my folks) for raising me creatively, giving me ample opportunities to be myself, believing in me always and dragging me round art galleries before I was able to walk. If it weren't for you I wouldn't be here today, and not just because you birthed me but because you saved me time and time again and for that I am ever grateful and full of love.

To the Mouthy Poets (RIP) for helping me grow as a poet and a person, I never thought it would be possible to become mouthier, but it happened.

To Write Minds A.K.A Hayley Green for letting me write openly about my suffering - encouraging me to pour my heart onto the paper and not filter out the blood, it's thanks to you I got up on my first open mic and haven't stopped since.

To My ex boy and girlfriends for filling and then breaking my heart and thus prompting me to write some of my most powerful pieces.

To Alex Milne for all the boogies, extended cuddles and reassurance that I'm doing okay.

To Stephen Thomas for being my partner in crime when It comes to the Nottingham poetry scene and helping me step out of my comfort zones when he knows I need to but am scared.

To my old therapist Laurence Baldwin for listening to the depressing poetry 15-year-old me couldn't stop splurging out, helping me get my autistic diagnosis and not giving up even when I'd given up on myself, I will never forget how much you cared.

To Ellie and Russ for helping me pick countless sets in the car journeys to poetry events, cooking me dinner and telling me when I'm being an absolute fool (I know it's often.)

To Bridie Squires for proving it's okay to swear in poetry.

To my cat for letting me bury my face in her belly when the world gets too much, sleeping on my chest every night and slobbering all over my journals to give them that weathered look every tumblr kid wanted in 2012.

To Holly Foster for being my best friend through thick and thin and always being on the other end of the phone.

To Chris McLoughlin for teaching me it's beautiful to be vulnerable, always appreciating my endless supply of dog pictures and editing the crap out of this collection (it needed doing!)

To Anne Holloway A.K.A the spine of Big White Shed for having faith in my ability, patience in my flakiness and giving me all the guidance and resources I needed to be able to produce this collection, I hope I've done you proud.